TONIER CAIN

RELATIONSHIPS
after
TRAUMA

JOURNAL

_____

YOUR NAME

Healing
NEEN

A Tonier Cain International Publication
P.O. Box 175 • Arnold, MD 21012

Co-Creators:: Tonier Cain, Desiráe G. Wright
Cover Design, Interior Layout: Christopher K. Wright

1

IDENTIFYING A TRAUMATIC PAST

—

*"Then the peace of God that exceeds
all understanding will keep your hearts
and minds safe in Christ Jesus."*

PHILIPPIANS 4:7

JOURNAL ASSIGNMENT #1

• Divide the page in two.

• On the left side list, your triggers.

• On the right side, list the tools you use to deal with each trigger.

Be honest with yourself. This is an exercise to help, not judge. It's alright if you don't know what triggers you or how to self-regulate. You can start identifying them now.

When you're faced with something that causes you fear, puts your senses on alert or kicks you into fight or flight mode; that's a trigger. Add it to your list.

What you find yourself doing after you've been triggered is how you cope. Add it to your list, then evaluate if your method of coping is healthy. If it's unhealthy, get help to develop healthy ways to self-regulate.

_____

DATE OF ENTRY

IDENTIFYING A TRAUMATIC PAST

TRIGGER	TOOL USED TO DEAL WITH THE TRIGGER

IDENTIFYING A TRAUMATIC PAST

TRIGGER	TOOL USED TO DEAL WITH THE TRIGGER

2

MOTHERHOOD

—

"Don't be anxious about anything: Rather,
bring upall of your requests to God in prayer and
petitions, along with giving thanks."

PHILIPPIANS 4:6

JOURNAL ASSIGNMENT #2

We are not responsible for the voids caused in our lives; however we have the power to fill them in healthy ways.

• Write down the positive ways you've learned to fill
  your voids

• Write down any voids you may still need to find healthy ways
  to satisfy

• Write down any unhealthy ways you fill voids

POSITIVE WAYS YOU'VE LEARNED TO FILL YOUR VOIDS

VOIDS YOU MAY STILL NEED TO FIND HEALTHY WAYS TO SATISFY

UNHEALTHY WAYS YOU FILL VOIDS

JOURNAL ASSIGNMENT #3

Have you ever made bad decisions for your child(ren) due to your trauma? If so:

• Write down how it impacted your child(ren)

_____

DATE OF ENTRY

BAD DECISIONS AND HOW THEY IMPACTED YOUR CHILDREN

_____

_____

_____

_____

_____

_____

_____

_____

_____

_____

_____

_____

_____

_____

_____

_____

_____

_____

_____

_____

_____

_____

_____

_____

JOURNAL ASSIGNMENT #4

Did you have secure or insecure attachments with your parent(s)?

Do you have secure or insecure attachments with your child(ren)?

• Write down what you've learned from these relationships that can help you be a better parent

_____

DATE OF ENTRY

WHAT YOU'VE LEARNED FROM THESE RELATIONSHIPS
THAT CAN HELP YOU BE A BETTER PARENT

3

EMPLOYEE

—

*"Lord God, you created heaven and earth
by your great power and outstretched arms;
nothing is too hard for you"*

JEREMIAH 32:17

JOURNAL ASSIGNMENT #5

Take a moment and think about a typical day at work,
then write your answers to the following questions:

• Do you feel your work environment is safe for a trauma
survivor? If so, what makes you feel that way?

• Do your co-workers know that you're a trauma survivor? If
not, do you think it's safe for them to know?

• Are there things that trigger you at work? If so, what?

• What are some things you do to help calm you?

• What calms you that you can you integrate into your work
day. For example, taking a walk to get fresh air or having a
cup of tea.

• What are some things you can do to help you feel safe at
work? For example, already have music in your office, keep
teas at your desk, or identifying someone at work you feel
safe to talk to.

DO YOU FEEL YOUR WORK ENVIRONMENT IS SAFE FOR A TRAUMA SURVIVOR? IF SO, WHAT MAKES YOU FEEL THAT WAY?

DO YOUR CO-WORKERS KNOW THAT YOU'RE A TRAUMA SURVIVOR?
IF NOT, DO YOU THINK IT'S SAFE FOR THEM TO KNOW?

ARE THERE THINGS THAT TRIGGER YOU AT WORK? IF SO, WHAT?

WHAT ARE SOME THINGS YOU DO TO HELP CALM YOU?

WHAT CALMS YOU THAT YOU CAN YOU INTEGRATE INTO YOUR WORK DAY?

WHAT ARE SOME THINGS YOU CAN DO TO HELP YOU FEEL SAFE AT WORK?

4

DATING

—

*"I am the Lord your God, who grasps
your strong hand, who says to you,
don't fear; I will help you"*

ISAIAH 41:13

JOURNAL ASSIGNMENT #6

True healing begins within. However, many of us are guilty of trying to find outward solutions to internal struggles. Are you placing that responsibility on the significant other in your life? Have you penalized a significant other for not being able to satisfy your internal needs? Take a moment to make amends in your journal.

• Write a letter taking accountability for unfair expectations you've placed on a significant other

• Write a letter to someone that you've been in a relationship with that placed unfair expectations on you

• Keep the letters and read, revise and add as needed

DATE OF ENTRY

A LETTER TO YOUR SIGNIFICANT OTHER

A LETTER TO SOMEONE THAT YOU'VE BEEN IN A RELATIONSHIP WITH THAT PLACED UNFAIR EXPECTATIONS ON YOU

5

MARRIAGE

—

"So then, they are no longer two but one flesh.
Therefore, what God has joined together,
let not man separate."

MATTHEW 19:6

JOURNAL ASSIGNMENT #7

Although marriage is a partnership it's important to hold on to your individuality to maintain a strong union. A well-balanced individual makes for a great partner, which establishes a firm foundation to build a healthy relationship.

• Write down the ways you pay attention to your own triggers

• Write down the ways you pay attention to spouse's triggers

• Write down the ways you pay attention to your marital needs

• Has it been hard for you to be intimate with your spouse

DATE OF ENTRY

WAYS YOU PAY ATTENTION TO THE NEEDS OF YOUR SPOUSE

WAYS YOU PAY ATTENTION TO YOUR MARITAL NEEDS

HAS IT BEEN HARD FOR YOU TO BE INTIMATE WITH YOUR SPOUSE?

6

FRIENDSHIP

—

*"A man who has friends must himself
be friendly, but there is a friend who sticks
closer than a brother."*

PROVERBS 18:24

JOURNAL ASSIGNMENT #8

Ask yourself, does what I see in people block me from getting close to them, or is it what I'm afraid they will see in me. Maybe it's a combination. Don't let your fears prevent you from experiencing the support and love of a true friend.

• Write down what causes you to distrust others

• Write down what you're afraid of others knowing about you

• Write about a time you haven't been a good friend

DATE OF ENTRY

WHAT CAUSES YOU TO DISTRUST OTHERS?

WHAT ARE YOU AFRAID OF OTHERS KNOWING ABOUT YOU?

A TIME YOU HAVEN'T BEEN A GOOD FRIEND

7

BUSINESS OWNER

—

"Commit your work to the Lord,
and your plans will succeed."

PROVERBS 16:3

JOURNAL ASSIGNMENT #9

We all know people who've let their past limit their expectations for their future. Have you allowed fear to block your success?

• Write down what you have yet to accomplish in life

• Write down obstacles you've faced reaching your goal(s)

• Write down your abilities that support reaching your goal(s)

_____

DATE OF ENTRY

WHAT HAVE YOU YET TO ACCOMPLISH IN LIFE?

_____
_____
_____
_____
_____
_____
_____
_____
_____
_____
_____
_____
_____
_____
_____
_____
_____
_____
_____
_____
_____
_____
_____
_____

OBSTACLES YOU'VE FACED REACHING YOUR GOAL(S)

ABILITIES THAT SUPPORT REACHING YOUR GOAL(S)

8

CHILD OF GOD

—

"But those who did welcome him,
those who believed in his name, he authorized
to become God's children."

JOHN 1:12

JOURNAL ASSIGNMENT #10

Now that you've finished the book, write a letter to yourself reminding you of the important points you want to remember

- Do you plan on applying anything from the book? If so, what?

- Has the book helped you let go of anything in your life? if so, what?

- Has the book provided you tools to improve your relationships, if so, what?

- Include anything else you found empowering and helpful to you moving forward

_____

DATE OF ENTRY

DO YOU PLAN ON APPLYING ANYTHING FROM THE BOOK? IF SO, WHAT?

HAS THE BOOK HELPED YOU LET GO OF ANYTHING IN YOUR LIFE? IF SO, WHAT?

HAS THE BOOK PROVIDED YOU TOOLS TO IMPROVE YOUR RELATIONSHIPS? IF SO, WHAT?

INCLUDE ANYTHING ELSE YOU FOUND EMPOWERING AND HELPFUL
TO YOU MOVING FORWARD

H**O**PE

For booking information, email
hello@toniercain.com

www.toniercain.com

Follow us on social media,
@toniercain

Made in the USA
Middletown, DE
04 January 2021